Book & CD for B♭, E♭, Bass Clef and C instruments

VOLUME
5

PLAY 8 SONGS WITH A
PROFESSIONAL BAND

HOW TO USE THE CD:

Each song has two tracks:

1) Full Stereo Mix

All recorded instruments are present on this track.

2) Split Track

Piano and **Bass** parts can be removed
by turning down the volume on the LEFT channel.

Guitar and **Horn** parts can be removed
by turning down the volume on the RIGHT channel.

Cover photo © Camera Press, LT / Retna, LTD

ISBN 978-1-4234-8670-1

7777 W. BLUEMOUND RD. P.O. BOX 13819 MILWAUKEE, WI 53213

Visit Hal Leonard Online at
www.halleonard.com

B.B. KING

BOOK

CD

C Versions

Everyday I Have the Blues
Words and Music by Peter Chatman

Additional Lyrics

2. Well, nobody loves me, nobody seems to care.
   Oh, nobody loves me, nobody seems to care.
   Well, worries and trouble, darling,
   Babe, you know I've had my share. Oh, look out!

4. Oh, no one loves me, nobody seems to care.
   Whoa, nobody loves me, nobody seems to care.
   Hey, now, worries and trouble, darlin',
   Babe, you know I've had my share.

It's My Own Fault Darlin'

Words and Music by B.B. King and Jules Bihari

8

Additional Lyrics

2. Well, you used to say that you loved me,
   But you be around with the boys.
   Now you're gonna leave me,
   Goin' to Pe'ria, Illinois.
   My own fault, darlin',
   If you wanna treat me the way you do.
   Yes, when you were lovin' me, baby,
   I kept tryin' to go, I didn't love you.

Please Accept My Love

Words and Music by B.B. King and Saul Bihari

YOUR __ LOVE __ I'LL CHER-ISH TO MY GRAVE. ____ AND IF YOU DIE __ BE-
FORE I DO, I'LL __ END MY LIFE ____ TO BE ____ WITH YOU.

BRIDGE

I'M LIKE THE PIC-TURE ON _____ THE WALL. __ PLEASE ____ DON'T __
LET ____ ME FALL. ____ IT'S MY HEART I'M THINK-IN' OF. __
WON'T YOU PLEASE, PLEASE, PLEASE __ AC-CEPT MY LOVE? 4. IF YOU LET ME BE __ YOUR __

VERSE

SLAVE, __ YOUR __ LOVE __ I'LL CHER-ISH TO MY GRAVE. ____
AND ____ IF YOU __ DIE BE - FORE ____ I DO, _____
I'LL END MY LIFE TO BE WITH YOU. _____

ADDITIONAL LYRICS

2. IF YOU ONLY, ONLY KNEW
JUST HOW MUCH I LOVE YOU.
LOVING YOU THE WAY THAT I DO,
YOU'D TAKE TONIGHT TO LOVE ME TOO.

11

Sweet Sixteen

Words and Music by B.B. King and Joe Bihari

CD TRACK
- ⑤ Full Stereo Mix
- ⑬ Split Mix

C Version

Intro
Medium shuffle ♩. = 60

1. When I first met you, ba - by,
2.-6. See additional lyrics

ba - by, ___ you were just ___ sweet six - teen. ___

First met you. ___ ba - by, ___

Lord, ___ you were just ___ sweet six - teen. ___

6th time, To Coda ⊕

you'd just left your home ___ then, ___ ba - by. Oh, the

1., 2.

sweet - est thing ___ I'd ev - er seen. ___

Copyright © 1967 by Universal Music - Careers
Copyright Renewed
International Copyright Secured   All Rights Reserved

12

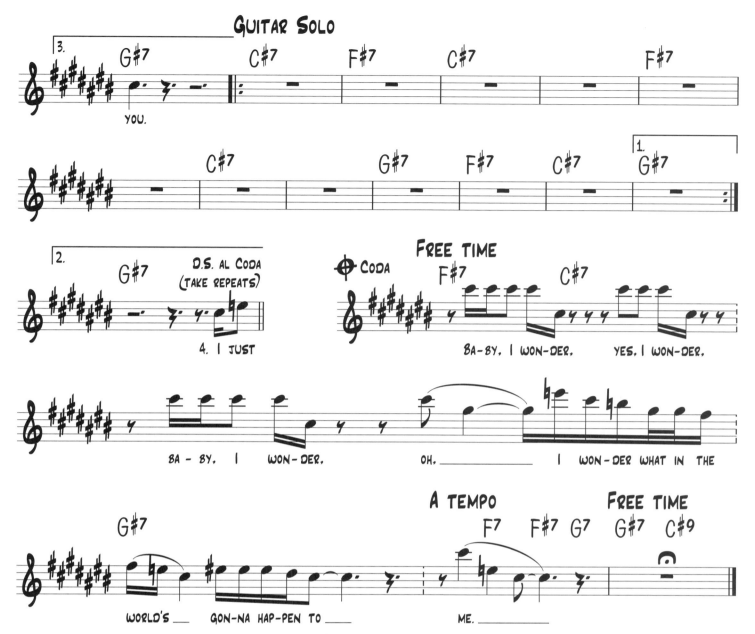

ADDITIONAL LYRICS

2. BUT YOU WOULDN'T DO NOTHING, BABY,
   YOU WOULDN'T DO ANYTHING I ASKED YA TO.
   YOU WOULDN'T DO NOTHIN' FOR ME, BABY,
   OH, YOU WOULDN'T DO ANYTHING I ASKED YOU TO.
   YOU KNOW YOU RAN AWAY FROM YOUR HOME, BABY,
   AND NOW YOU WANNA RUN AWAY FROM OLD B, TOO.

3. YOU KNOW I LOVE YOU, BABE,
   AND I'LL DO ANYTHING YOU TELL ME TO.
   YOU KNOW, YOU KNOW I LOVE YOU, BABY,
   BABY, I LOVE YA AND I'LL DO ANYTHING YA TELL ME TO.
   NOTHING IN THE WORLD, BABY,
   LORD, THERE AIN'T NOTHING,
   NOTHING IN THE WORLD I WOULDN'T DO FOR YOU.

4. I JUST GOT BACK FROM VIETNAM, BABY,
   AND YA KNOW I'M A LONG, LONG WAY FROM NEW ORLEANS.
   OH, I JUST GOT BACK FROM VIETNAM, BABY,
   OH BABY, AND I'M A LONG, LONG WAY FROM NEW ORLEANS.
   I'M HAVING SO MUCH PROBLEMS, BABY,
   BABY, I WONDER WHAT IN THE WORLD IS GONNA HAPPEN TO ME.

5. TREAT ME MEAN, BABY,
   BUT I'LL KEEP ON LOVING YOU JUST THE SAME.
   OH, TREAT ME MEAN, TREAT ME MEAN, BABY,
   I'LL KEEP ON LOVING YOU, KEEP ON LOVING YOU JUST THE SAME.
   BUT ONE OF THESE DAYS, BABY,
   YOU'RE GONNA GIVE A LOT OF MONEY
   TO HEAR SOMEONE CALL MY NAME. OH!

6. YOU'RE SWEET SIXTEEN, BABY, SWEET SIXTEEN.
   OH, YES, THE SWEETEST THING, BABY,
   OH, YES, THE SWEETEST THING I EVER SEEN.
   YES, YOU KNOW I'M HAVING SO MUCH TROUBLE PEOPLE.
   BABY, I WONDER....

The Thrill Is Gone
Words and Music by Roy Hawkins and Rick Darnell

INTRO
Moderately slow ♩ = 88

VERSE

1. The thrill is gone, the thrill is gone a-way.
2., 3. See additional lyrics

The thrill is gone, ba-by, the thrill is gone a-way.

You know you done me wrong, ba-by, and you'll be sor-ry some day.

1.
2. be. D.S. AL CODA

⊕ CODA
should.

VERSE

Bm

4. You know I'm ____ free, free now, ____ ba - by. I'm free ____ from your ____ spell.

Em

Whoa, I'm free, ____ free, free ____ now, I'm free ____

Bm

____ from your spell.

Gmaj⁷

And now ____ that it's all o - ver

F♯7

Bm

all I can do ____ is wish you ____ well. ____

OUTRO-Guitar Solo

Bm   Em   Bm

Gmaj⁷   F♯7   Bm   Bm   **Repeat and Fade**

Additional Lyrics

2. The thrill is gone,
It's gone away from me.
The thrill is gone, baby,
The thrill has gone away from me.
Although I'll still live on,
But so lonely I'll be.

3. The thrill is gone,
It's gone away for good.
Oh, the thrill is gone,
Baby, it's gone away for good.
Someday I know I'll be holdin' on, baby,
Just like I know a good man should.

Why I Sing the Blues

Words and Music by B.B. King and Dave Clark

INTRO
Moderately ♩ = 120

1. Ev - 'ry-bod - y wants to know _____ why ___ I
2. - 6. See additional lyrics

sing the blues. ___ Yes, I ___ say ___ ev-'ry-bod-y wan-na know

why ___ I sing the blues. ___ Well, I've been a-

6th time, To Coda ⊕

round a long ___ time. I real-ly have ___ paid ___ my dues.

Guitar Solo

Outro-Guitar Solo

Additional Lyrics

2. When I first got the blues, they brought me over on a ship.
   Men were standin' over me and a lot more with the whip.
   And ev'rybody wanna know why I sing the blues.
   Well, I've been around a long time. Mm, hmm, I've really paid my dues.

3. I've laid in the ghetto flats, cold and numb.
   I heard the rats tell the bedbugs to give the roaches some.
   Ev'rybody wanna know why I'm singin' the blues.
   Yes, I've been around a long time. People, I've paid my dues.

4. I stood in line down at the county hall.
   I heard a man say, "We're gonna build some new apartments for y'all."
   And ev'rybody wanna know, yes, they wanna know why I'm singin' the blues.
   Yes, I've been around a long, long time. Yes, I've really, really paid my dues.
   Now I'm gonna play Lucille.

5. My kid's gonna grow up, gonna grow up to be a fool.
   'Cause they ain't got no more room, no more room for him in school.
   And ev'rybody wanna know, ev'rybody wanna know why I'm singin' the blues.
   I say, I've been around a long time. Yes, I've really paid some dues.

6. Yeah, you know the company told me, "Guess you're born to lose."
   Ev'rybody around me, people, it seem like ev'rybody got the blues.
   But I had 'em a long time. I've really, really paid my dues.
   You know, I ain't ashamed of it, people. I just love to sing my blues.

You Upset Me Baby

Words and Music by B.B. King and Jules Bihari

INTRO
Medium Shuffle ♩ = 114

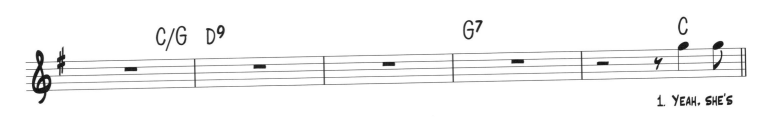

18

YES, I'M TELL - IN' YOU PEO - PLE. ___ SHE'S SOME-THING FINE ___

THAT YOU REAL-LY OUGHT TO SEE. ___

2. WELL, SHE'S

GUITAR/SAXOPHONE SOLO

4. WELL, I'VE

DO TO ME. ___

ADDITIONAL LYRICS

2. WELL, SHE'S NOT TOO TALL, COMPLEXION IS FAIR.
   MAN, SHE KNOCKS ME OUT THE WAY SHE WEARS HER HAIR.
   YOU UPSETS ME, BABY. YES, YOU UPSETS ME, BABY.
   LIKE BEIN' HIT BY A FALLIN' TREE, WOMAN, WOMAN, WHAT YOU DO TO ME.

3. WELL, I'VE TRIED TO DESCRIBE HER, IT'S HARD TO STOP.
   I BETTER STOP NOW BECAUSE I GOT A WEAK HEART.
   YOU UPSETS ME. WELL, YOU UPSETS ME, BABY.
   WELL, LIKE BEIN' HIT BY A FALLIN' TREE, WOMAN, WHAT YOU DO TO ME.

4. WELL, I'VE TRIED TO DESCRIBE HER, IT'S HARD TO STOP.
   I BETTER STOP NOW BECAUSE I GOT A VERY WEAK HEART.
   YOU UPSETS ME, BABY. YES, YOU UPSETS ME, BABY.
   WELL, LIKE BEIN' HIT BY A FALLIN' TREE, WOMAN, WHAT YOU DO TO ME.

Just Like a Woman

By B.B. King

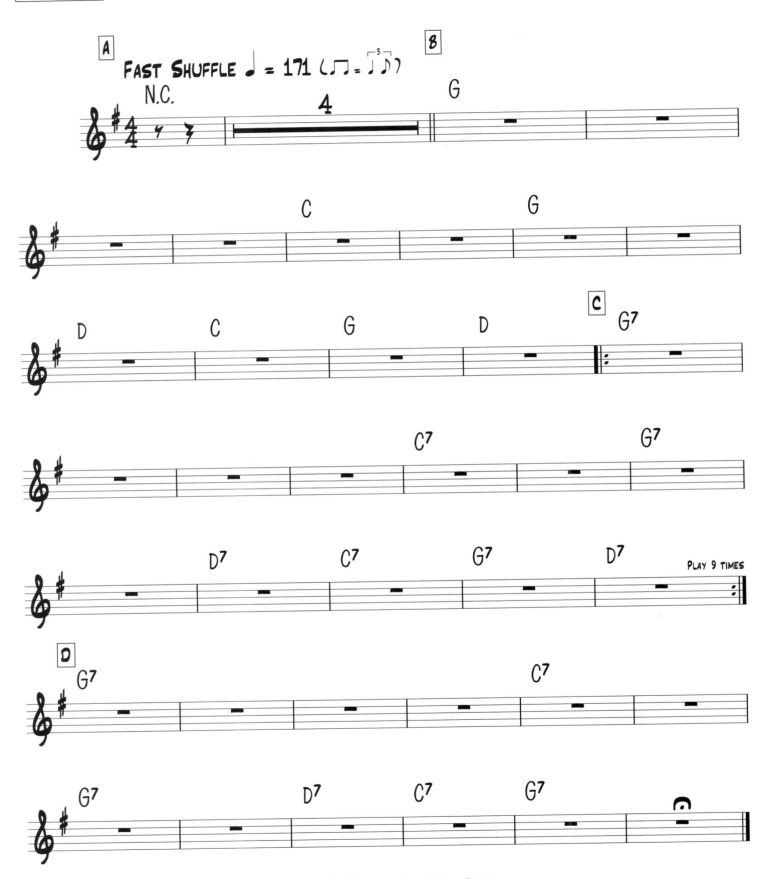

B^b VERSIONS

Everyday I Have the Blues

Words and Music by Peter Chatman

INTRO
MODERATE SHUFFLE ♩ = 105

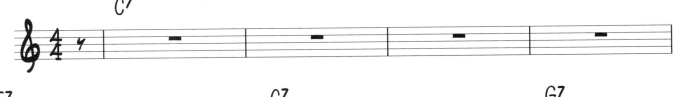

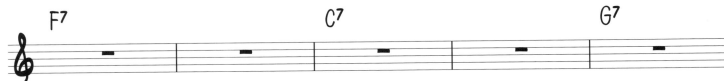

VERSE

1. Ev - 'ry day,
2. See additional lyrics

Ev - 'ry day I have the blues. ___ Oh. ___

___ Ev - 'ry day, ___ Ev - 'ry day I have the blues. ___

When you see me wor - ry, babe. ___ yeah. ___ it's you I

1.   2.   GUITAR SOLO

hate _ to lose. ___ 2. Well, ___ Oh, ___ look out!

Additional Lyrics

2. WELL, NOBODY LOVES ME, NOBODY SEEMS TO CARE.
OH, NOBODY LOVES ME, NOBODY SEEMS TO CARE.
WELL, WORRIES AND TROUBLE, DARLING,
BABE, YOU KNOW I'VE HAD MY SHARE. OH, LOOK OUT!

4. OH, NO ONE LOVES ME, NOBODY SEEMS TO CARE.
WHOA, NOBODY LOVES ME, NOBODY SEEMS TO CARE.
HEY, NOW, WORRIES AND TROUBLE, DARLIN',
BABE, YOU KNOW I'VE HAD MY SHARE.

It's My Own Fault Darlin'

Words and Music by B.B. King and Jules Bihari

VERSE

3. YES, _____ I'M GON - NA GO. _____

YES, I'M GON - NA LET YOU HAVE YOUR WAY.   YOU'RE HAV - IN' YOUR GOOD _ TIMES NOW, BA - BY.

I'M __ GON - NA HAVE __ A HOL - I - DAY. __ IT'S MY __

OWN FAULT, _ DAR - LIN',   IF YOU WAN - NA TREAT ME _____ THE WAY YOU DO.

YES, WHEN YOU, _ AH, ___ YOU WERE LOV - IN' ME, BA - BY,

I KEPT ___ TRY - IN' TO GO, _____ I DID - N'T

LOVE YOU. _____

ADDITIONAL LYRICS

2. WELL, YOU USED TO SAY THAT YOU LOVED ME,
BUT YOU BE AROUND WITH THE BOYS.
NOW YOU'RE GONNA LEAVE ME,
GOIN' TO PE'RIA, ILLINOIS.
MY OWN FAULT, DARLIN',
IF YOU WANNA TREAT ME THE WAY YOU DO.
YES, WHEN YOU WERE LOVIN' ME, BABY,
I KEPT TRYIN' TO GO, I DIDN'T LOVE YOU.

Please Accept My Love
Words and Music by B.B. King and Saul Bihari

Additional Lyrics

2. If you only, only knew
   Just how much I love you.
   Loving you the way that I do,
   You'd take tonight to love me too.

Sweet Sixteen
Words and Music by B.B. King and Joe Bihari

Intro
Medium shuffle ♩. = 60

% Verse

1. When I first met you, ba - by,
2.-6. See additional lyrics

Ba - by, ___ you were just ___ sweet six - teen. ___

First met you, ___ ba - by, ___

Lord, ___ you were just _____ sweet six - teen. ___

6th time. To Coda

You'd just left your home _____ then, ___ ba - by.   Oh, the

1., 2.

Sweet-est thing _____ I'd ev - er seen. ___

Additional Lyrics

2. But you wouldn't do nothing, baby,
You wouldn't do anything I asked ya to.
You wouldn't do nothin' for me, baby,
Oh, you wouldn't do anything I asked you to.
You know you ran away from your home, baby,
And now you wanna run away from old B, too.

3. You know I love you, babe,
And I'll do anything you tell me to.
You know, you know I love you, baby,
Baby, I love ya and I'll do anything ya tell me to.
Nothing in the world, baby,
Lord, there ain't nothing,
Nothing in the world I wouldn't do for you.

4. I just got back from Vietnam, baby,
And ya know I'm a long, long way from New Orleans.
Oh, I just got back from Vietnam, baby,
Oh baby, and I'm a long, long way from New Orleans.
I'm having so much problems, baby,
Baby, I wonder what in the world is gonna happen to me.

5. Treat me mean, baby,
But I'll keep on loving you just the same.
Oh, treat me mean, treat me mean, baby,
I'll keep on loving you, keep on loving you just the same.
But one of these days, baby,
You're gonna give a lot of money
To hear someone call my name. Oh!

6. You're sweet sixteen, baby, sweet sixteen.
Oh, yes, the sweetest thing, baby,
Oh, yes, the sweetest thing I ever seen.
Yes, you know I'm having so much trouble people.
Baby, I wonder....

The Thrill Is Gone
Words and Music by Roy Hawkins and Rick Darnell

VERSE

4. You know I'm ___ free, free now, ___ ba - by. I'm free _ from your _ spell.

Whoa, I'm free, _ free, free ___ now, I'm free ___

___ from your spell. And now ___ that it's all o - ver ___

all I can do ___ is wish you _ well. ___

Outro-Guitar Solo

C#m   F#m   C#m

Amaj7   G#7   C#m   C#m   Repeat and Fade

Additional Lyrics

2. The thrill is gone,
   It's gone away from me.
   The thrill is gone, baby,
   The thrill has gone away from me.
   Although I'll still live on,
   But so lonely I'll be.

3. The thrill is gone,
   It's gone away for good.
   Oh, the thrill is gone,
   Baby, it's gone away for good.
   Someday I know I'll be holdin' on, baby,
   Just like I know a good man should.

Why I Sing the Blues

Words and Music by B.B. King and Dave Clark

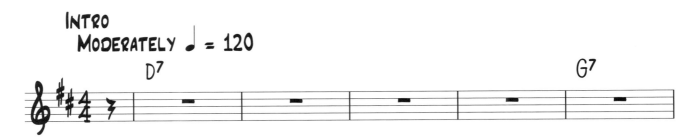

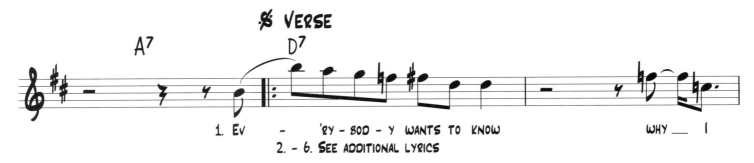

1. Ev - 'ry-bod - y wants to know why I

2. - 6. See additional lyrics

sing the blues. Yes, I say ev-'ry-bod-y wan-na know

why I sing the blues. Well, I've been a-

round a long time. I real-ly have paid my dues.

Guitar Solo

Additional Lyrics

2. When I first got the blues, they brought me over on a ship.
   Men were standin' over me and a lot more with the whip.
   And ev'rybody wanna know why I sing the blues.
   Well, I've been around a long time. Mm, hmm, I've really paid my dues.

3. I've laid in the ghetto flats, cold and numb.
   I heard the rats tell the bedbugs to give the roaches some.
   Ev'rybody wanna know why I'm singin' the blues.
   Yes, I've been around a long time. People, I've paid my dues.

4. I stood in line down at the county hall.
   I heard a man say, "We're gonna build some new apartments for y'all."
   And ev'rybody wanna know, yes, they wanna know why I'm singin' the blues.
   Yes, I've been around a long, long time. Yes, I've really, really paid my dues.
   Now I'm gonna play Lucille.

5. My kid's gonna grow up, gonna grow up to be a fool.
   'Cause they ain't got no more room, no more room for him in school.
   And ev'rybody wanna know, ev'rybody wanna know why I'm singin' the blues.
   I say, I've been around a long time. Yes, I've really paid some dues.

6. Yeah, you know the company told me, "Guess you're born to lose."
   Ev'rybody around me, people, it seem like ev'rybody got the blues.
   But I had 'em a long time. I've really, really paid my dues.
   You know, I ain't ashamed of it, people. I just love to sing my blues.

You Upset Me Baby

Words and Music by B.B. King and Jules Bihari

INTRO
Medium shuffle ♩ = 114

1. YEAH, SHE'S

THIR-TY-SIX IN THE BUST.
2., 3., 4. See additional lyrics
TWEN-TY-EIGHT IN THE WAIST,

FOR-TY-FOUR IN THE HIPS, SHE GOT A, REAL ___ CRA - ZY LEGS.

YOU UP-SETS ___ ME, BA - BY.   YES.   YOU UP-SETS ME, BA - BY.

Additional Lyrics

2. Well, she's not too tall, complexion is fair.
   Man, she knocks me out the way she wears her hair.
   You upsets me, baby. Yes, you upsets me, baby.
   Like bein' hit by a fallin' tree, woman, woman, what you do to me.

3. Well, I've tried to describe her, it's hard to stop.
   I better stop now because I got a weak heart.
   You upsets me. Well, you upsets me, baby.
   Well, like bein' hit by a fallin' tree, woman, what you do to me.

4. Well, I've tried to describe her, it's hard to stop.
   I better stop now because I got a very weak heart.
   You upsets me, baby. Yes, you upsets me, baby.
   Well, like bein' hit by a fallin' tree, woman, what you do to me.

Just Like a Woman

By B.B. King

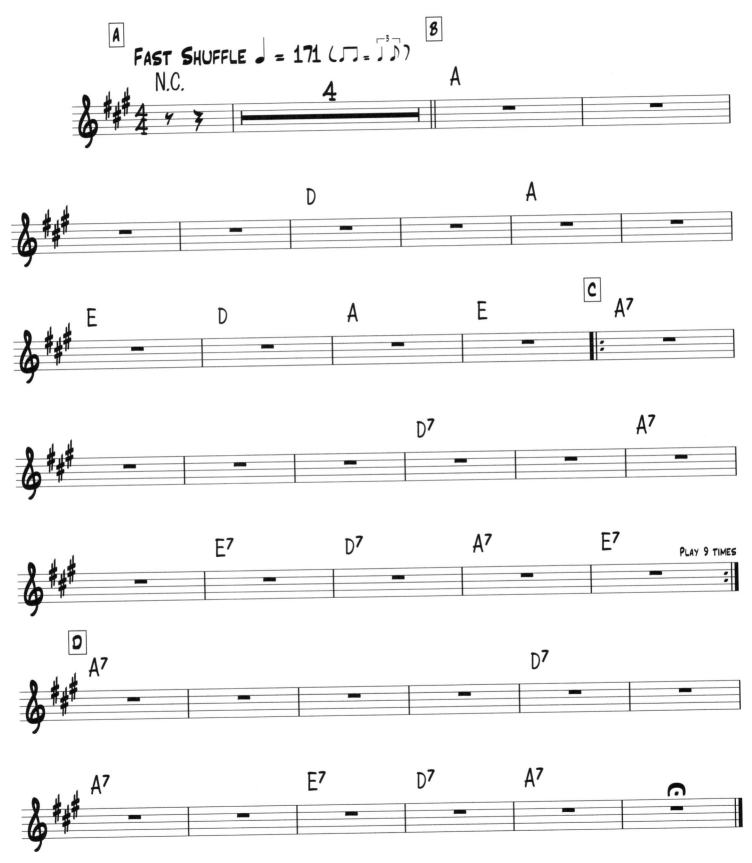

E♭ VERSIONS

Everyday I Have the Blues

Words and Music by Peter Chatman

Additional Lyrics

2. Well, nobody loves me, nobody seems to care.
Oh, nobody loves me, nobody seems to care.
Well, worries and trouble, darling,
Babe, you know I've had my share. Oh, look out!

4. Oh, no one loves me, nobody seems to care.
Whoa, nobody loves me, nobody seems to care.
Hey, now, worries and trouble, darlin',
Babe, you know I've had my share.

E♭ Version

It's My Own Fault Darlin'

Words and Music by B.B. King and Jules Bihari

INTRO
Slowly ♩. = 68

VERSE

1. WELL, IT'S MY OWN FAULT, DAR-LIN', IF YOU WAN-NA TREAT ME THE WAY YOU DO.
2. SEE ADDITIONAL LYRICS

YEAH, IT'S MY OWN FAULT, BA - BY, IF YOU WAN-NA TREAT ME THE WAY YOU DO.

YES, WHEN YOU WERE LOV-IN' ME, BA-BY, I KEPT TRY-IN' TO GO,

1. I DID-N'T LOVE YOU.
2. LOVE YOU.

GUITAR SOLO

Additional Lyrics

2. Well, you used to say that you loved me,
   But you be around with the boys.
   Now you're gonna leave me,
   Goin' to Pe'ria, Illinois.
   My own fault, darlin',
   If you wanna treat me the way you do.
   Yes, when you were lovin' me, baby,
   I kept tryin' to go, I didn't love you.

YOUR _ LOVE _ I'LL CHER-ISH TO MY GRAVE. _____ AND IF YOU DIE ___ BE

FORE I DO. ___ I'LL ___ END MY LIFE ___ TO BE ____ WITH YOU.

BRIDGE

I'M LIKE THE PIC-TURE ON _____ THE WALL. ___ PLEASE ____ DON'T

___ LET ___ ME FALL. _____ IT'S MY HEART I'M THINK-IN' OF. ___

___ WON'T YOU PLEASE, PLEASE, PLEASE _ AC-CEPT MY LOVE? 4. IF YOU LET ME BE _ YOUR _

VERSE

___ SLAVE. __ YOUR _ LOVE _ I'LL CHER-ISH TO MY GRAVE. _____

AND ___ IF YOU ___ DIE BE - FORE _____ I DO. ___

I'LL ___ END MY LIFE TO BE WITH YOU. _____

ADDITIONAL LYRICS

2. IF YOU ONLY, ONLY KNEW
JUST HOW MUCH I LOVE YOU.
LOVING YOU THE WAY THAT I DO,
YOU'D TAKE TONIGHT TO LOVE ME TOO.

43

Sweet Sixteen

Words and Music by B.B. King and Joe Bihari

Additional Lyrics

2. But you wouldn't do nothing, baby,
You wouldn't do anything I asked ya to.
You wouldn't do nothin' for me, baby,
Oh, you wouldn't do anything I asked you to.
You know you ran away from your home, baby,
And now you wanna run away from old B, too.

3. You know I love you, babe,
And I'll do anything you tell me to.
You know, you know I love you, baby,
Baby, I love ya and I'll do anything ya tell me to.
Nothing in the world, baby,
Lord, there ain't nothing,
Nothing in the world I wouldn't do for you.

4. I just got back from Vietnam, baby,
And ya know I'm a long, long way from New Orleans.
Oh, I just got back from Vietnam, baby,
Oh baby, And I'm a long, long way from New Orleans.
I'm having so much problems, baby,
Baby, I wonder what in the world is gonna happen to me.

5. Treat me mean, baby,
But I'll keep on loving you just the same.
Oh, treat me mean, treat me mean, baby,
I'll keep on loving you, keep on loving you just the same.
But one of these days, baby,
You're gonna give a lot of money
To hear someone call my name. Oh!

6. You're sweet sixteen, baby, sweet sixteen.
Oh, yes, the sweetest thing, baby,
Oh, yes, the sweetest thing I ever seen.
Yes, you know I'm having so much trouble people.
Baby, I wonder....

E♭ VERSION

The Thrill Is Gone
WORDS AND MUSIC BY ROY HAWKINS AND RICK DARNELL

VERSE

G#m 4. You know I'm ___ free, free now. ___ Ba - by. I'm free _ from your _ spell.

C#m Whoa, I'm free. _ free, free _____ now, I'm free ___

G#m ___ from your spell. **Emaj7** And now ___ that it's all o - ver _____

D#7 All I can do _____ **G#m** is wish you _ well. _____

OUTRO-GUITAR SOLO

G#m   **C#m**   **G#m**

Emaj7 **D#7** **G#m**   **G#m**   *REPEAT AND FADE*

ADDITIONAL LYRICS

2. The thrill is gone,
   It's gone away from me.
   The thrill is gone, baby,
   The thrill has gone away from me.
   Although I'll still live on,
   But so lonely I'll be.

3. The thrill is gone,
   It's gone away for good.
   Oh, the thrill is gone,
   Baby, it's gone away for good.
   Someday I know I'll be holdin' on, baby,
   Just like I know a good man should.

Why I Sing the Blues

Words and Music by B.B. King and Dave Clark

Intro
Moderately ♩ = 120

1. Ev - 'ry-bod - y wants to know why I

2. - 6. See additional lyrics

sing the blues. Yes, I say ev-'ry-bod-y wan-na know

why I sing the blues. Well, I've been a-

round a long time. I real-ly have paid my dues.

6th time, To Coda ⊕

Additional Lyrics

2. When I first got the blues, they brought me over on a ship.
   Men were standin' over me and a lot more with the whip.
   And ev'rybody wanna know why I sing the blues.
   Well, I've been around a long time. Mm, hmm, I've really paid my dues.

3. I've laid in the ghetto flats, cold and numb.
   I heard the rats tell the bedbugs to give the roaches some.
   Ev'rybody wanna know why I'm singin' the blues.
   Yes, I've been around a long time. People, I've paid my dues.

4. I stood in line down at the county hall.
   I heard a man say, "We're gonna build some new apartments for y'all."
   And ev'rybody wanna know, yes, they wanna know why I'm singin' the blues.
   Yes, I've been around a long, long time. Yes, I've really, really paid my dues.
   Now I'm gonna play Lucille.

5. My kid's gonna grow up, gonna grow up to be a fool.
   'Cause they ain't got no more room, no more room for him in school.
   And ev'rybody wanna know, ev'rybody wanna know why I'm singin' the blues.
   I say, I've been around a long time. Yes, I've really paid some dues.

6. Yeah, you know the company told me, "Guess you're born to lose."
   Ev'rybody around me, people, it seem like ev'rybody got the blues.
   But I had 'em a long time. I've really, really paid my dues.
   You know, I ain't ashamed of it, people. I just love to sing my blues.

You Upset Me Baby

Words and Music by B.B. King and Jules Bihari

YES, I'M TELL-IN' YOU PEO-PLE,___ SHE'S SOME-THING FINE _

___ THAT YOU REAL-LY OUGHT TO SEE. ___ 2. WELL, SHE'S

Guitar/Saxophone Solo

4. WELL, I'VE

DO TO ME. ___

Additional Lyrics

2. Well, she's not too tall, complexion is fair.
   Man, she knocks me out the way she wears her hair.
   You upsets me, baby. Yes, you upsets me, baby.
   Like bein' hit by a fallin' tree, woman, woman, what you do to me.

3. Well, I've tried to describe her, it's hard to stop.
   I better stop now because I got a weak heart.
   You upsets me. Well, you upsets me, baby.
   Well, like bein' hit by a fallin' tree, woman, what you do to me.

4. Well, I've tried to describe her, it's hard to stop.
   I better stop now because I got a very weak heart.
   You upsets me, baby. Yes, you upsets me, baby.
   Well, like bein' hit by a fallin' tree, woman, what you do to me.

JUST LIKE A WOMAN

By B.B. King

CD TRACK
- ③ Full Stereo Mix
- ⑪ Split Mix

E♭ Version

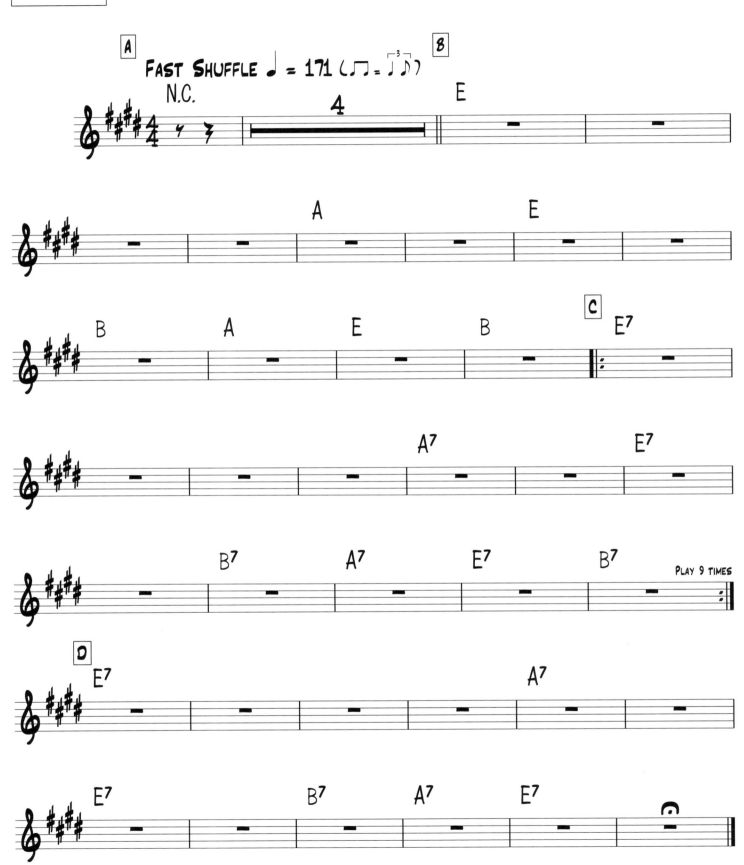

𝄢 C VERSIONS

Everyday I Have the Blues

Words and Music by Peter Chatman

C Version

ADDITIONAL LYRICS

2. WELL, NOBODY LOVES ME, NOBODY SEEMS TO CARE.
   OH, NOBODY LOVES ME, NOBODY SEEMS TO CARE.
   WELL, WORRIES AND TROUBLE, DARLING,
   BABE, YOU KNOW I'VE HAD MY SHARE. OH, LOOK OUT!

4. OH, NO ONE LOVES ME, NOBODY SEEMS TO CARE.
   WHOA, NOBODY LOVES ME, NOBODY SEEMS TO CARE.
   HEY, NOW, WORRIES AND TROUBLE, DARLIN',
   BABE, YOU KNOW I'VE HAD MY SHARE.

It's My Own Fault Darlin'

Words and Music by B.B. King and Jules Bihari

♭ C Version

ADDITIONAL LYRICS

2. WELL, YOU USED TO SAY THAT YOU LOVED ME,
   BUT YOU BE AROUND WITH THE BOYS.
   NOW YOU'RE GONNA LEAVE ME,
   GOIN' TO PE'RIA, ILLINOIS.
   MY OWN FAULT, DARLIN',
   IF YOU WANNA TREAT ME THE WAY YOU DO.
   YES, WHEN YOU WERE LOVIN' ME, BABY,
   I KEPT TRYIN' TO GO, I DIDN'T LOVE YOU.

Please Accept My Love

Words and Music by B.B. King and Saul Bihari

ADDITIONAL LYRICS

2. If you only, only knew
   Just how much I love you.
   Loving you the way that I do,
   You'd take tonight to love me too.

Sweet Sixteen

Words and Music by B.B. King and Joe Bihari

CD TRACK
5 Full Stereo Mix
13 Split Mix

C Version

Additional Lyrics

2. But you wouldn't do nothing, baby,
You wouldn't do anything I asked ya to.
You wouldn't do nothin' for me, baby,
Oh, you wouldn't do anything I asked you to.
You know you ran away from your home, baby,
And now you wanna run away from old B, too.

3. You know I love you, babe,
And I'll do anything you tell me to.
You know, you know I love you, baby,
Baby, I love ya and I'll do anything ya tell me to.
Nothing in the world, baby,
Lord, there ain't nothing,
Nothing in the world I wouldn't do for you.

4. I just got back from Vietnam, baby,
And ya know I'm a long, long way from New Orleans.
Oh, I just got back from Vietnam, baby,
Oh baby, And I'm a long, long way from New Orleans.
I'm having so much problems, baby,
Baby, I wonder what in the world is gonna happen to me.

5. Treat me mean, baby,
But I'll keep on loving you just the same.
Oh, treat me mean, treat me mean, baby,
I'll keep on loving you, keep on loving you just the same.
But one of these days, baby,
You're gonna give a lot of money
to hear someone call my name. Oh!

6. You're sweet sixteen, baby, sweet sixteen.
Oh, yes, the sweetest thing, baby,
Oh, yes, the sweetest thing I ever seen.
Yes, you know I'm having so much trouble people.
Baby, I wonder,...

The Thrill Is Gone
Words and Music by Roy Hawkins and Rick Darnell

INTRO %
Moderately slow ♩ = 88

1. The thrill is gone. ___
2., 3. See additional lyrics

The thrill is gone ___ a-way. ___

The thrill is gone, ___ ba - by,

The thrill is gone ___

___ a - way. ___

You know you done me wrong, ___ ba -

- by, and you'll ___ be sor - ry some day. ___

To Coda

1.

2. D.S. al Coda

___ be.

Coda

should.

VERSE

4. YOU KNOW I'M ___ FREE, FREE NOW. ___ BA - BY.   I'M FREE ___ FROM YOUR ___ SPELL.

WHOA, I'M ___ FREE. ___ FREE, FREE _____ NOW.   I'M FREE ___

___ FROM YOUR SPELL.   AND NOW ___ THAT IT'S ALL O - VER ___

ALL I CAN DO _____ IS WISH YOU ___ WELL. ___

OUTRO-GUITAR SOLO

REPEAT AND FADE

ADDITIONAL LYRICS

2. THE THRILL IS GONE,
   IT'S GONE AWAY FROM ME.
   THE THRILL IS GONE, BABY,
   THE THRILL HAS GONE AWAY FROM ME.
   ALTHOUGH I'LL STILL LIVE ON,
   BUT SO LONELY I'LL BE.

3. THE THRILL IS GONE,
   IT'S GONE AWAY FOR GOOD.
   OH, THE THRILL IS GONE,
   BABY, IT'S GONE AWAY FOR GOOD.
   SOMEDAY I KNOW I'LL BE HOLDIN' ON, BABY,
   JUST LIKE I KNOW A GOOD MAN SHOULD.

Why I Sing the Blues

Words and Music by B.B. King and Dave Clark

INTRO
MODERATELY ♩ = 120

1. Ev - 'ry - bod - y wants to know   why __ I

2. - 6. See additional lyrics

sing the blues. __   Yes, I __ say __ ev-'ry-bod-y wan-na know

why __ I   sing   the   blues. __   Well, I've been a-

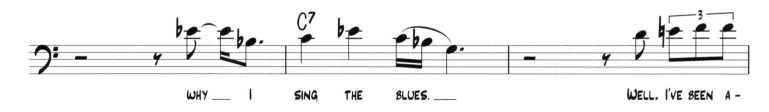

round a long __ time.   I real-ly have __ paid __ my dues.

Guitar Solo

2. When I

D.S. al Coda
(take repeat)

Coda

5. My

Outro-Guitar Solo

Begin Fade

Fade Out

Additional Lyrics

2. When I first got the blues, they brought me over on a ship.
Men were standin' over me and a lot more with the whip.
And ev'rybody wanna know why I sing the blues.
Well, I've been around a long time. Mm, hmm, I've really paid my dues.

3. I've laid in the ghetto flats, cold and numb.
I heard the rats tell the bedbugs to give the roaches some.
Ev'rybody wanna know why I'm singin' the blues.
Yes, I've been around a long time. People, I've paid my dues.

4. I stood in line down at the county hall.
I heard a man say, "We're gonna build some new apartments for y'all."
And ev'rybody wanna know, yes, they wanna know why I'm singin' the blues.
Yes, I've been around a long, long time. Yes, I've really, really paid my dues.
Now I'm gonna play Lucille.

5. My kid's gonna grow up, gonna grow up to be a fool,
'Cause they ain't got no more room, no more room for him in school.
And ev'rybody wanna know, ev'rybody wanna know why I'm singin' the blues.
I say, I've been around a long time. Yes, I've really paid some dues.

6. Yeah, you know the company told me, "Guess you're born to lose."
Ev'rybody around me, people, it seem like ev'rybody got the blues.
But I had 'em a long time. I've really, really paid my dues.
You know, I ain't ashamed of it, people. I just love to sing my blues.

You Upset Me Baby

Words and Music by B.B. King and Jules Bihari

INTRO
MEDIUM SHUFFLE ♩ = 114

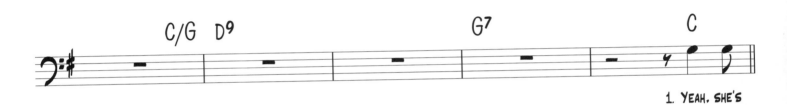

1. YEAH, SHE'S

𝄉 VERSE

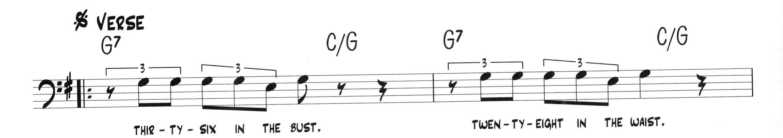

THIR - TY - SIX IN THE BUST, TWEN - TY-EIGHT IN THE WAIST,

2., 3., 4. See additional lyrics

FOR - TY - FOUR IN THE HIPS, SHE GOT A REAL ___ CRA - ZY LEGS.

YOU UP - SETS ___ ME, BA - BY. YES, YOU UP - SETS ME, BA - BY.

Guitar/Saxophone Solo

Additional Lyrics

2. Well, she's not too tall, complexion is fair.
   Man, she knocks me out the way she wears her hair.
   You upsets me, baby. Yes, you upsets me, baby.
   Like bein' hit by a fallin' tree, woman, woman, what you do to me.

3. Well, I've tried to describe her, it's hard to stop.
   I better stop now because I got a weak heart.
   You upsets me. Well, you upsets me, baby.
   Well, like bein' hit by a fallin' tree, woman, what you do to me.

4. Well, I've tried to describe her, it's hard to stop.
   I better stop now because I got a very weak heart.
   You upsets me, baby. Yes, you upsets me, baby.
   Well, like bein' hit by a fallin' tree, woman, what you do to me.

Just Like a Woman

By B.B. King

𝄢 C Version

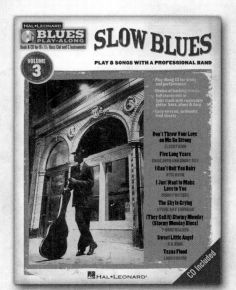

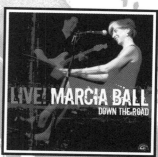